Disclaimer

Nick Marr © 2019 – All Rights Reserved

© Nick Marr 2019

No part of this eBook may be reproduced, stored, or transmitted in any form or by any means including mechanical or electronic without prior written permission from the author.

While the author has made every effort to ensure that the ideas, statistics, and information presented in this eBook are accurate to the best of his abilities, any implications direct, derived, or perceived, should only be used at the reader's discretion. The author cannot be held responsible for any personal or commercial damage arising from communication, application, or misinterpretation of information presented herein.

All Rights Reserved.

Acknowledgment

I'm eternally grateful...

To my wife, Jane, who supports me as a serial entrepreneur. Without her I would not have been able to develop the businesses that have created. They provided me with leadership skills and business experience that has been crucial in my own self development.

To my children, Alex & Hayley, who have helped me become a better person by allowing me to see myself from another perspective.

To my inspirational father Ian who, despite the challenges of the time, married my mother Shirley. There mixed-race marriage in the 1960's proves that love conquers all.

To my brother Graham and my sister Sonia whose love is always there.

To the Metropolitan Police Leadership Academy where I began my life coaching and in particular to Carl Daeche who created, designed, and implemented all Metropolitan Police Service (MPS) leadership and management development programs.

To Sally Burrows of Bridges International Ltd, her advice and experience as a first-class coach and mentor have served to develop me as a successful coach.

To Steve Kay, a Master NLP Practitioner and the Author of 'Become a Great Leader & Coach Using NLP' He provides such in-depth knowledge based on years of experience helped me bring my coaching to another level.

Table of Contents

Manage interruptions

Don't Leave Things Unfinished

Be a Change Warrior

Acknowledge Your Weaknesses

Adopt The Pareto Principle

Concentrate on the circle of influence

It's All in Your Hands!

Nick Marr BIO

Nick Marr is an author, speaker and executive coach with a passion for inspirational leadership. He started his coaching career as a police officer, helping to deliver a change to senior officer leadership styles.

He also represented minority police officers in various roles throughout his 20-year career. His move into business saw him as founder of one of the first online estate agencies in the UK. He has worked as Chief Marketing Officer and Vice President of Sales for Digital Marketing organisations.

His innovation in business led to him being featured in the Financial Times and appearances on BBC TV.

Author's Note

Welcome to my eBook!

Being a coach is a lifelong journey of learning and teaching, so I take it upon myself to disseminate knowledge and ideas that can help you bring positive changes in your life. It is my personal observation that a large number of motivated workers are always in search of ways to enhance their performance at work. This is exactly what this book is about!

I made it my business to find a better way of working. My success as an entrepreneur, founder, and coach meant I needed to learn how to optimise my performance to maintain the quality of work required in my various roles.

It's time I share what I learned along the way. I have dedicated this book to reveal strategies, tips, and tricks to help high performing individuals perform work-related tasks in a better manner without having to clock-in additional hours!

Isn't it the ultimate millennial dream – to work more in less time? The strategies discussed in this book are the sum of independent research and my own experience in this field.

The studies that I have discussed and quoted in my eBook are mentioned below.

- https://www.mckinsey.com/business-functions/organization/our-insights/why-diversity-matters
- https://www.apa.org/pubs/journals/releases/xhp274763.pdf

Good luck to all!

All around the world, millions of people are working the wrong way. Their bosses are encouraging them, new employees are being trained the wrong way, and there is no formal education to help employees be the best version of themselves at work. In other words, there's chaos out there. Although employees are working day in and out, they fail to reach their full potential, leading to mediocre performance, additional effort, and less work.

However, I have never coached anyone who wanted to work longer hours. Therefore, it is really important that we make the most out of the precious time that we commit to working. If you are working really hard and are investing a lot of time in your work, I can help you achieve better performance without increasing your work hours.

My coaching is all about enjoying the journey. We only have one life so let's make the most of it by employing some better tactics to achieve more with less effort. Let's take a look at some of the most effective strategies that can help you be more productive at work!

Examine Your Values

Have you ever reflected your true values? Do you know what really drives you? Examining your personal values is a powerful exercise and can be a part of successful goal setting. Knowing what makes you tick will help you be more successful.

Whether you are in an organisation or running your own business, if your work conflicts with your personal values, you are unlikely to benefit from the strategies I will suggest later. It makes sense – when your values are aligned with the work you do, you are bound to perform your best!

Get someone to write your values down one by one until you struggle to think of anymore. Tucked far away in your subconscious, you will unearth your hidden values and priorities. Here's a list of some values you may want to consider.

- Dependability
- Reliability
- Loyalty
- Commitment
- Open-mindedness
- Consistency
- Honesty
- Fairness
- Good humour
- Compassion
- Motivation
- Positivity
- Optimism
- Passion
- Respect

- Fitness

Research shows that work performance is directly related to overall satisfaction in life. This means, the better you perform at work, the better life you will live! This is because fewer working hours with more success allows you to meet most of your goals. Also, you will be able to invest more time in family, friends, or anything else you consider important in your life. All this can be achieved by figuring out your most prioritized values in order to understand what drives you to work better.

Number One Rule – 'Do Less Work'!

Yes, you read that right! One of the biggest secrets that I am going to explain to you is that you need to do less! To up your game and to become a top performer, you need to improve your focus and try to put your work efforts into fewer tasks.

Don't just take my word for it, the facts speak for themselves!

Morten T. Hansen, who is a Harvard Business School and INSEAD (France), a professor with a Ph.D. from Stanford Business School, created an in-depth study involving 5,000 workers. His academic research has won several prestigious awards, and is ranked as one of the world's most influential management thinkers by Thinkers50.

He found that the best-performing people did less but they were obsessed about the tasks they had. This created high performing individuals. The study shows that when people acted on a 'do less and obsess" strategy, the effect was substantial. In fact, people who mastered this technique scored 25% higher in terms of performance than those who did not follow the same method of work.

According to Daniel Goldman and Stephen Cover, people can only perform at their best if they select a few items to work on and say no to others. Morten Hansen says that "Picking a few priorities is only half the equation. The other half is the requirement that you must obsess over your chosen area of focus to excel."

This means that instead of trying to take care of as much work as you can, a better strategy is to choose a single or only a few tasks and make them your first priority, focusing entirely on them!

Identify High Impact and Low Impact

I learned some valuable lessons from Steve Kay, a Master Neuro-Linguistic Practitioner (NLP) and accomplished author of "Become A Great Leader & Coach using NLP". He simplified the process of focus by splitting your tasks into High Impact and Low Impact.

I want you to think about the real purpose of your job. What is your organizational role and why does it exist? Think broader. Why is your job even required? Now that you know the importance of your organizational role, it is time to identify the tasks that have the biggest impact on your job. What are the things you are doing that will really make the most impact?

Make separate lists for high-impact tasks and the low-impact tasks. Once you have the lists, it's time to analyse these activities. Make sure your judgement is not biased. Don't let the fun part of your job or "I-have-always-done-it-that-way" mentality affect your judgment. This is an important exercise for you to reach optimal performance.

Questions to Ask Yourself

1. What are the low priority, low impact activities that take a lot of your time? What can you do to eliminate the temptation to spend time on these activities?

2. What are the high priority, low impact activities that you should be delegating to someone else? How much of your time is spent in this segment?

How much of this time could you reallocate to high impact activities?

3. Reanalyse – Are all of the activities in your high impact segment high impact? Do some of them really belong in a lower category but get put into this category because the activity feels really, really productive? Is there even 5% of your time there you could reclaim if you wanted to perform at a much higher level?

4. How much of your time is spent in the low priority, high impact activity segment? What kind of results could you produce if you doubled that time?

Now that you have the list, think about how much time you are spending on Low Impact vs. High Impact activities. It does not make sense for you to be spending the majority of your time on low impact activities. You will need to be proactive to change the status quo.

High Performance Comes from Sequential Tasking

Are you good at multitasking? Or do you prefer doing jobs sequentially? If you are a fan of multitasking, I am going to present you with some evidence that may help you rethink.

A huge [study](#) of nearly 60,000 court cases before judges in Milan, Italy found that judges who handled cases simultaneously by multitasking took longer to complete than other judges who performed them a case at a time. In fact, the difference was enormous.

While the cases were randomly assigned, the judges' performance was rated on the same workload. Researchers found that more than 50% of the total increases when multitasking approach was employed. On average, the slowest judge spent 398 days to close all the cases while the fastest took only 178 days or less than half the time.

Cognitive research has verified that people are incapable of multitasking. Yes, almost anyone can walk and chew gum at the same time. But for any task that takes cognitive function such as thinking, writing, speaking, planning or designing, we actually switch-task. We switch back and forth between tasks. That's why talking on the phone and driving at the same time leads to dangerous incidents we've all seen like swerving, driving through red lights, or veering across multiple lanes to get to a missed exit.

Our brain takes time to switch from one activity to another, especially for highly complex tasks. For instance, for new product development, an average brain can take 20 minutes to get back into a highly productive flow. However, most of us struggle to get 20 minutes of uninterrupted work, which means we rarely get into the zone.

Additionally, when you switch tasks, you often forget some part of what you had been working on previously. It becomes easy to miss out on important details. Compound this with frequent switching throughout the day and it's a wonder anything ever gets done.

Don't Fall for this Working Trap

Anyone who can't say no to accepting more tasks is setting themselves up to fail. People who get overwhelmed by taking on multiple tasks are falling into the trap. They work harder, for longer hours. However, at the end of the day, they fail to perform at their best.

It's a thankless task, others will view your performance as mediocre, failing to appreciate that you are doing so many things. What's more is that as you work harder on more tasks, the pressure and stress eventually adds up. This is neither good for you or for your business at large. You may look to leave, end up having an outburst, or worse.

In order to build a successful career and maintain it, you need to start saying no more often so that you can stay focused and instead of wasting time on low impact tasks, you can invest your efforts on the high impact priorities.

Here's when and how you can politely decline to take up additional responsibilities at work.

When Old School Thinking Is Common

You may be working with a boss or a team that believe the more work you take, the harder you are working. However, that's far from reality. In fact, this old way of thinking is a flawed strategy affecting the performance of individuals worldwide. Keep in mind, as discussed earlier, management experts believe that people achieve their best by focusing on fewer activities.

When You Are Good at What You Do

High achievers are likely to become the "go to" person in any organization. Every time a new task arrives, everyone is going to look up to them! The bosses will want to hand the task to the people they know will get the job done to a great standard. The trouble is that if you are that person it will hurt your performance.

If your boss or colleague asks you to take on additional work and you can't handle it, say so. Explain diplomatically why you can't take on the work, and ask what the other person needs and why. Then try to find a win-win solution that works for all. This will enhance both parties' awareness of the other's workload, as well as set the tone for future time management and division of responsibilities. They will also see that you have a high work ethic and want to produce the best you can.

How to Increase Performance through Member Meetings

When you are focused on high impact activities and a meeting invite arrives, it's time to start thinking differently. If you can't think of a clear goal for the meeting to accomplish, or your goal could be achieved by another method, there's no need to hold the meeting in the first place!

Keep in mind that unorganized member meetings can take time away from your focused activities. Here's what you can do to avoid this from happening.

Always Have an Agenda

Save time in your meetings and get everyone on the same page (literally) by creating a meeting agenda in advance. During the meeting, use your agenda as a roadmap to keep the conversation on the topic. This is an easy way to make productive use of your time and effectively achieve your goals.

Best to have a Moderator

When it comes to having effective meetings, a moderator can make all the difference. The main job of a moderator is to make sure that everyone gets a chance to speak their mind. They also need to intervene when a member starts rambling and wasting the time of the group. A moderator will keep the meeting on target and make sure it does not go off the tangent.

Be Punctual

Manage everyone's expectations by making sure that the meeting starts and ends at the appointed times. On your agenda, set aside the last five to ten minutes for discussing everyone's next steps after the meeting. Make sure you leave the meeting with action steps. Otherwise, what was the point of getting in the room in the first place?

The moderator can proactively wrap the meeting up and make sure each person knows which action items they're responsible for. Also, keep your guest list exclusive.

Increase Efficiency with Diversity

When it comes to getting the best from a meeting, group thinking is the worst possible scenario. Creating an open culture where everyone enjoys equal opportunity to assist in coming up with a new way forward is essential.

A report by McKinsey&Company that covered 366 public companies in a variety of countries and industries found that the industries and organizations that were more diverse, ethnically and gender-wise, performed significantly better than the others.

The problem is that when you narrow the backgrounds, experiences, and outlooks of the people on your team, you are limiting the number of solutions that can be explored. At best, you will come up with fewer ideas and at worst, you run the risk of creating an echo chamber where inherent biases are normalized and groupthink sets in. I have always said two heads are better than one, especially when it comes to creative workplaces where innovation thrives.

By bringing together a diverse group of people, you can see the situation from differing perspectives. Sometimes we cannot see what's in front of us until someone who is not 100% familiar with the subject states the obvious.

Avoid the Glory

The great thing about diverse meeting groups is that one idea can be like an embryo. The entire group works together to develop the idea into something tangible. I remember, once, during a meeting I had what I thought was a fantastic idea. However, three other members added their contributions to it, creating a watered-down version of my original suggestion that proved invaluable.

Promote the Right Organizational Culture

By creating an open culture of ideas where everyone's idea and contribution is equal, you also motivate individuals and send them a valuable message of equality. You will also start to identify key individuals who have an abundance of common sense and creativity.

Listen Actively to Achieve More

To optimise your performance, you need to master your active listening skills. Texting or letting your mind wander when a person is speaking can adversely affect your listening skills. It is also disrespectful to the person speaking. Furthermore, the evidence about the effects of multitasking are clear. This means, when you are multitasking, you are less likely to comprehend and interpret the verbal information that you are receiving.

Active listeners hide the ego, respond to what's being said, and ponder on every statement. Always be open to new ideas and be conscious of your body language when they are coming from a colleague. Sometimes, people who have burning ideas may be highly sensitive at this important time. Receive the ideas with open arms and more will come.

It takes a lot of concentration and determination to be an active listener but in your quest to be a star performer, it will pay dividends. Old habits are hard to break, and if your listening skills are as bad as most people's, then you'll need to do a lot of work to break these bad habits.

There are four key techniques that you can use to develop your active listening skills. Let's take a look at them.

1. **Pay attention:** Give the speaker your undivided attention, and acknowledge the message.

2. **Show that you're listening**: Make sure that your posture is open and interested.

3. **Encourage the speaker:** Make small verbal comments like "yes" and "uh huh". Reflect on what has been said by paraphrasing. "What I'm hearing is...," and "Sounds like you are saying...," are great ways to reflect back.

4. **Defer judgment:** Allow the speaker to finish each point before asking questions. Don't interrupt with counter-arguments. Make sure you respond appropriately. Be candid, open and honest in your response. And most of all, assert your opinions respectfully.

Start using active listening techniques today to become a better communicator, improve your workplace productivity, and develop better relationships.

Have a Positive Attitude

In a meeting where ideas are being developed by a group, some suggestions will be discounted while others will be selected and appreciated. In some minds, this may mean winners and losers. It's really important to understand that once a decision has been agreed upon and everyone is behind the idea, there is nothing worse than demotivated team members. As a leader, you will need to use your emotional intelligence to see how team members are reacting.

Keep in mind that your attitude at work is important to your overall success. When you go into work, make sure you put on your best attitude as soon as you enter those doors. Just by staying positive, you're setting the trend for your co-workers to be positive too.

Although it's much easier to sit around and complain, this can negatively impact your own work – whether you want it to or not. In general, having a positive attitude just makes work better for everyone. Don't be a negative Nancy.

Show Your Passion

People around you love to work with someone who has positivity, drive, and passion. It is truly infectious. Furthermore, the colleagues who enjoy working with you will help you perform to your best. Going the extra mile for something you're passionate about will really help get the best out of you.

Important to Be Coachable

People who hang onto how many years' experience they have are good but when this is coupled with an open learning attitude, they become awesome. I am one of those people who love to explore new ideas and are never stuck in the past. In fact, I am always learning! Irrespective of who they are in the organisation, everyone can learn! The key is to never become too proud to learn from others.

In fact, listening and learning from a colleague not only helps you but they will also feel they are doing something worthwhile by explaining something they know. If you aren't coachable, that means you aren't open to learning new things and building on your skills. To your managers and your peers, this translates to appearing as if you're unwilling to better yourself or the company.

Your mind-set for performance should always be one of continual learning. Always be open to new experiences and different ways of doing things.

How to Stay Focused

I remember, once, back when I was in school, my school report said, "Nick is easily distracted in class". Thankfully, things have changed since then as I realised that a wandering mind is really the enemy within that needs to be eliminated.

When it comes to staying focused, it is important to understand that the ability to concentrate is like a muscle. The more you exercise, the more you go to the gym, the better developed your muscles are going to be.

If you're somebody who's constantly distracted, you are probably used to multitasking, and 40 minutes of focus time might be too much for you. So, start with 5. Get comfortable with 5 minutes of paying attention to only one task. Then make it 10, make it 15, make it 20! Slowly build your way up to about 40 to 50 minutes of focus time. Train your brain to remain focused.

You will need to learn to "Eat the Frog! Imagine you have a selection of delicious food on your plate, except for a great big slimy green frog. It needs to be eaten but you will always want to eat all the smaller more tastier food first and avoid the frog till last! The trouble is the frog will spoil the beautiful food you have just eaten. Leaving the frog till last has also spoilt your enjoyment as you become more anxious as you clear your plate.

Inability to prioritise will result in you taking on too much work. You don't like to say 'No', so you accept any task that is asked of you. Rather than focus on one task at a time, you try to please everybody by jumping from one task to another. The end result is that you get nothing done. Before long, you have developed a large to-do list which is frightening to look at. The thought of completing the to-do list is so overwhelming and painful that you have no idea where to begin. You really don't want to think about it so, in order to avoid it; you distract yourself with meaningless tasks. This allows you to feel busy but you get nothing accomplished.

Mornings are the Best

Everyone knows themselves the best. For example, I know I work harder and can be in the zone during mornings. In fact, instead of starting a new job in the late afternoon, I usually put it aside for the next morning as I know it will be a high-quality job in the morning.

Surely, I am not alone. Most of us have more energy, willpower, and the drive to tackle the harder tasks in the morning. For this reason, it is advisable to complete your high impact, high demand work in the mornings while you are still fresh.

Decision-Making is Draining

Your focus and willpower get depleted every single time you need to make a decision – the decisions don't need to be important ones either! It can be a decision about what to wear today, or about what to eat. Every little decision chips away at your willpower, at your focus, and at your energy. The closer you get it to the morning, the more focus you're going to have, the more concentration you're going to have, the easier it will be to actually stay focused.

Never Work During Lunch Breaks

To maintain high performance, you need regular breaks. So, when it is time for lunch, get up and move away from the place you are working at. Always take lunch away from your computer and out of your working seat.

When you eat lunch in front of your computer, your brain doesn't get a chance to switch off, and regroup. The result – an afternoon characterized by foggy thinking, tiredness, and diminished productivity. Stepping away at lunch can help your brain fire on all cylinders.

It is important to understand that there's an element of refreshment that a different environment, particularly an external environment can bring. A change is as good as a rest and returning to work after your lunch break will serve to have you feel invigorated and refuelled.

Admitting that you need a break is not a weakness, it just means you're aware of your limitations, and you're wise enough to admit it. It is all part of your self-care, which I coach to help the best people become more resilient. We live in a society where taking breaks and relaxation is not "cool" because you're expected to be "on-duty" 24/7. However, taking breaks is going to allow your focus to renew.

Keep in mind that your energy follows a very predictable pattern every single day: it goes up, and it takes about 2 ½ hours to go down. And when your energy starts going down, so does your focus, your concentration, your willpower, and even your mood. This makes it important to always get off your seat during the lunch break. The core problem with working longer hours is that time is a finite resource. Energy is a different story. Defined in physics as the capacity to work, energy comes from four main wellsprings in human beings: the body, emotions, mind, and spirit. In each, energy can be systematically expanded and regularly renewed by establishing specific rituals—behaviours that are intentionally practiced and precisely scheduled, with the goal of making them unconscious and automatic as quickly as possible

Manage Interruptions

According to some of the most productive professionals in the world, "distractions" are the biggest enemy of productivity. Every time you feel tempted to waste some time checking on Facebook or catching on your favourite YouTube channels, remember what's at stake.

Interruptions can come in different forms. However, learning how to avoid them is vital to improve work performance. Even a small interruption can make you lose focus and waste time that you previously allocated to a task. This, in turn, increases the risk of your projects running late.

Don't Leave Things Unfinished

New Year's resolutions, diets, a new sport...they're all great for a while. However, after a while, it is common to just let it slip, and they go straight back to your to-do list!

There are a lot of solutions to procrastination, from finding the right times for your mind to engage in creative work to dividing a job into smaller tasks in order to avoid being overwhelmed by the complexity. Some people thrive on procrastination. If you typically come up with your best ideas during crunch time, don't feel as though you must do it some other way.

Make a habit of recording every project that you complete. One way to make sure you pick on this habit is to reward yourself for every project you complete!

Be a Change Warrior

Change is the only constant thing in life. Since it is always around us, it's time to embrace it now. In fact, be the one who instigates change from a new process to a new business idea.

It keeps your mind alert, fresh and full of ideas. People who look out for new ideas and are always on the watch to find what their competitors are doing are ahead of the game. They have a head start and perform well. They are not content with the status quo and bring new perspectives to meetings and eventually help everyone grow.

But what do you have to do to become the change warrior? Well, start by evaluating your work performance on a frequent basis. Keep your goals and responsibilities in mind every time you have to make a decision. Talk to your colleagues and listen to what they have to say.

Don't ever settle for mediocrity. Stay restless and always believe that everything can be at least 1% better than it was yesterday.

Change the way you deal with emails.

One study found that 1 in 3 office workers suffers from email stress. Making a decision the first time you open an email is crucial for good time management.

Emma advises practising the "4 Ds":

- **Delete:** you can probably delete half the emails you get immediately.

- **Do:** if the email is urgent or can be completed quickly.

- **Delegate:** if the email can be better dealt with by someone else.

- **Defer:** set aside time later to spend on emails that will take longer to deal with

Acknowledge Your Weaknesses

Feedback, they say, is a gift and people who seek it use it to improve performance. There's no way for a person to be good at everything. While we all have strengths and weaknesses, the great thing about acknowledging your weak spots is that is an easy way to identify easy improvement opportunities.

Self-reflection leads to self-improvement. When things are going well, ask yourself how you can contribute to making it better. On the other hand, when things take a turn for the south, ask yourself, "Did I make a wrong decision? What was my part in this? How can I make it better?" Capturing both good and bad will help you become the best version of yourself.

Adopt The Pareto Principle

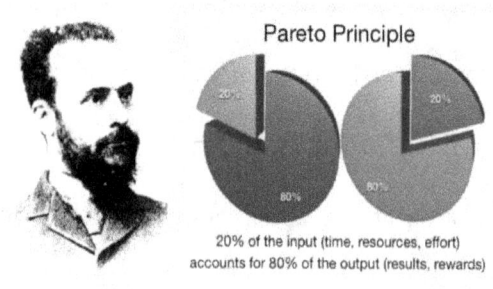

Pareto Principle

20% of the input (time, resources, effort) accounts for 80% of the output (results, rewards)

Originally, the Pareto Principle referred to the observation that 80% of Italy's wealth belonged to only 20% of the population. This principle is often referred to as the 80/20 rule . As the story goes, the origins of the 80/20 rule date back to 1906 when Pareto observed that 80% of the property in Italy was owned by 20% of the population. It should be noted that it was actually Joseph M. Juran who later generalized and named this rule[2], and thus, Juran should be credited with the principle's popularity and widespread use.

More generally, the Pareto Principle is the observation (not law) that **most things in life are not distributed evenly**. It can mean all of the following things:

- 20% of the input creates 80% of the result

- 20% of the workers produce 80% of the result

- 20% of the customers create 80% of the revenue

- 20% of the bugs cause 80% of the crashes

- 20% of the features cause 80% of the usage

- And on and on...

But be careful when using this idea! First, there's a common misconception that the numbers 20 and 80 must add to 100 — they don't!

20% of the workers could create 10% of the result. Or 50%. Or 80%. Or 99%, or even 100%. Think about it — in a group of 100 workers, 20 could do all the work while the other 80 goof off. In that case, 20% of the workers did 100% of the work. Remember that the 80/20 rule is a rough guide about **typical distributions**.

Also recognize that the numbers don't have to be "20%" and "80%" exactly. The key point is that **most things in life (effort, reward, output) are not distributed evenly – some contribute more than others**.

80 % of your distractions comes from 20% of sources.

To take on those distractions and eliminate them, you must first identify them. Your list may look something like this:

- Flurries of emails

- Incoming phone calls

- Unplanned visitors

- Thirst or hunger

- Social media notifications

After you have your list of distractions, review it and see which ones interrupt you the most. You will likely find that only two or three (20 percent) are the bulk (80 per cent) of the problem. Then incorporate ways to eliminate those interruptions. Here are some suggestions:

- Block specific times to work on emails.

- Let non-urgent calls go to voicemail.

- Close your office door.

- Have a drink and snack handy.

- Stay away from social media during work.

Time is Precious

TIME IS PRECIOUS

Waste it wisely

Time is our most precious resource; it's universally equating since we all have the same amount of time in our day. But most of us don't use that time efficiently. We have productivity peaks when we're most effective at whatever it is that we do. There are certain tasks, times of day, or even days of the week when we tend to produce the best results. So, by identifying these productivity peaks, and applying the 80/20 rule, we can optimally harness time and catapult our results.

Does this really work?

Yes. If you're able to identify which 20% of your causes are producing 80% of the results, you could magnify your results exponentially by harnessing this principle. Once you've identified the 20% of the causes, you can devote more of your time to those causes, thus expanding your results. This applies to finances, time-management, project management, and virtually every other area of life.

The 80/20 Rule in Time Management

The 80/20 Rule is a perfect fit for time management. As soon as you come to terms with the fact that input and output aren't a 1:1 proposition, it makes perfect sense why there's never enough time in the day.

Twenty per cent of your efforts will quickly eat up 80 per cent of your time, which means no matter how much sleep you skip or how much coffee your drink, you'll never get it all done.

If you want to make the most of your time, try applying the Pareto Principle by tackling the most important 20 per cent of your tasks first, without letting the pesky 80 per cent you can put off till later get in your way.

As someone who works from home, the easiest way I've found to prioritize things and stay on top of my own work commitments is to make sure my paid work is the 20 per cent I start with every day before moving on to any household tasks like washing dishes and mopping floors. The dishes and floors will still be there when I'm done writing, and they're not paying my bills, and if I don't frontload that critical 20 per cent, I'll be up all night trying to make up for it.

How to Be Proactive To Make Change Happen

Learning some new techniques is great but what is the use if they are not actively put into action. To make changes actually happen make sure you are a procative person. I mean examine what drives you with the aim of making meaningful change

Our attitudes and behaviors can often be discovered by our language in fact when coaching its sometime the language people use is a way to discover what's going on with their inner thoughts

How proactive are you many people who are reactive can step out of personal responsibility saying things like

"That's me its just way I am" – They are saying there is no way I can change and my habits are formed that's it

"My boss makes me angry" – Hold on your in control of your feeling you have chosen to be angry. Your saying its not your responsibility and that its outside your control

"I can do that I just don't have the time" Here your saying you have no control of your life and that it is that what is in charge not you

"If only my colleagues were more patient " Someone else behavior is limiting my effectiveness

"I have to do it that way" Other people are forcing you what to do you have no freedom to chose your own methods

Proactive people language

Proactive language, in contrast to reactive language, differs in terms of the locus of control experienced by the speaker. When someone has a sense of control over the situation, his speech generally reflects his control or acceptance of responsibility. The word selection and sentence patterns generally reveal insight into the way the speaker feels regarding the subject he is speaking about. Proactive language shows the speaker taking responsibility for a situation or experience, and seizing control as demonstrated by the use of active and decisive sentences.

Accepting Responsibility

Proactive language shows a clear acceptance of responsibility. People who use specific definitive statements are considered to be using proactive language while general, non-specific statements are considered more "reactive" than proactive. For example, someone who generalizes with statements like "I just can't" or "There is nothing I can do" or "I don't have time" is not taking responsibility for the situation. More appropriate, proactive statements would be "I will" or "I can."

Taking Control

Reactive statements, such as "If only..." claims, appear to be more effective at displaying the speaker as a victim of other people or external events. Proactive language shows the speaker is in control. Rather than saying, "If only I had a better job ..." or "If I had a better education ...," the proactive speaker says, "I don't like this job, I'm looking for a new one" and "I'm returning to school," then actually follows up the statements with actions to get a new job or return to school. The proactive speaker recognizes that life's events are not up to chance; they can be controlled simply by stepping up and taking that control.

Concentrate on the Circle of Influence

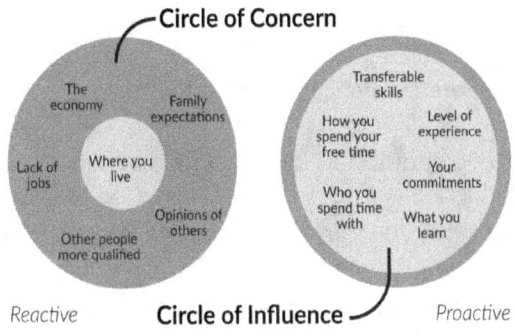

The model is based on two circles. The first is our circle of concern. This includes a whole range of things – global warming, the state of the economy, the clothes your children want to wear, attitudes in society, the organisation you work for, the things your colleagues do, the way people drive their cars etc. The actual list will depend on the individual, but the important thing to understand is that there may be little you can do about many of these things since they are outside your influence. Devoting energy on them may be a waste of time – the equivalent of shouting at the television – and time and energy once spent cannot be reused. Our circle of influence will be much smaller. It includes the things we can do something about. The key is to focus your energy on those things that you can influence – this will enable you to make effective changes. If you do this you will find your circle of influence starts to increase – others will see you as an effective person and this will increase your power. Conversely, if all your energy goes into those things you cannot change your circle of influence will shrink. Not only will you drain your energy, other people may start to see you as unduly negative and critical. Knowing how far your circle of influence extends is an important aspect of personal effectiveness. So is forming partnerships and alliances – you may not have any direct influence over something in your Circle of Concern, but you may know other people who do. A team can have a wider circle of influence than an individual. So reactive people find their circle of influence shrinks, while proactive people find that it increases.

Case Study - Expanding your influence will help you be successful

(source Harvard Business Review)

Marcy Shinder, chief marketing officer at Work Market, the New York City–based firm that helps businesses manage their freelancers and consultants, was working on establishing herself as an influential member of the team before she even started the job.

Before her first day of work, she arranged to meet several colleagues for informal coffees and lunches – one-on-one meetings that were "more personal, less structured, and allowed us to establish rapport." "I went in with a listening agenda," she explains. "I wanted to learn: What are their goals? What is important to them? What do they think is working at the company? And what do they want me to accomplish?"

Marcy made sure her body language conveyed that she was fully focused on these conversations. She sat up straight, made eye contact, and looked open and engaged. "Body language is so important — we coach salespeople on it," she says. "I tried to listen with intent."

Those early meetings allowed her to understand the perspectives, personalities, and motives of her colleagues, which proved to be useful when she recently had an idea to revamp the company's website and needed their support to move forward.

Thanks to those early one-on-one conversations, she could customize her pitch to each individual. For example, with Stephen Dewitt, the CEO, she talked about the company's vision. With Jeff Wald, the president and COO, an analytic thinker, she started with the metrics. And with the chief customer officer, she focused on the customer side.

"It is the same story, just with a different emphasis," she says. Her efforts paid off. The new Work Market website will go live this spring.

Another way Marcy increases her influence is by staying up-to-date on industry trends and news. "I spend 25% of my time talking to customers, other chief marketing officers, people on boards of companies, potential customers, and mentoring young people," she says. "By doing that, I stay informed and I have a finger on the pulse of what's happening beyond the four walls of this company."

To read more about Circles of Influence, I strongly recommend the "7 Habits of Highly Effective People" written by Stephen Covey

It's All in Your Hands!

You grow and learn new things every time something changes. You discover new insights about different aspects of your life.

Changes trigger progress and make you step out of the comfort zone.

To adopt some or all of the changes I have written about test your imagination by thinking of how it will look, the new efficient you. Imagine waking up and how your day will unfold and the successes that you have. Think it and believe it like its already happened.

The ability to envision in your mind what you cannot at present see with your eyes. It is based on the principle that all things are created twice.

There is a mental (first) creation, and a physical (second) creation.

The physical creation follows the mental, just as a building follows a blueprint. If you don't make a conscious effort to visualize who you are and what you want in life, then you empower other people and circumstances to shape you and your life by default. It's about connecting again with your own uniqueness and then defining the personal, moral, and ethical guidelines within which you can most happily express and fulfil yourself.

I hope this book will help you change so that things move forward and develop because of the them.

You learn lessons even from changes that did not lead you to where you wanted to be.

Throughout this eBook, I revealed some fantastic tried and tested techniques that works effectively for the most successful people. I hope that you benefit from them as well and follow them to get the most from your working day. In the end, it's only in your hands. Better yourself today, for a better tomorrow!

www.ingramcontent.com/pod-product-compliance
Lightning Source LLC
Chambersburg PA
CBHW051331220526
45468CB00004B/1594

9781797061528